EXPLORING
LIFE
CYCLES

Ladybugs

Aaron Carr

www.av2books.com

AV2

Step 1
Go to **www.av2books.com**

Step 2
Enter this unique code

IGXCBXBRH

Step 3
Explore your interactive eBook!

AV2

EXPLORING **LIFE** CYCLES

Ladybugs

Start!

AV2 is optimized for use on any device

Your interactive eBook comes with...

View new titles and product videos at
www.av2books.com

EXPLORING LIFE CYCLES

Ladybugs

CONTENTS

All animals begin life, grow, and have babies.

This is called a life cycle.

Ladybugs are insects.
Insects are small
animals with six legs.

An insect has its skeleton
on the outside of its body.

Ladybugs **hatch** from eggs.

The eggs look like small jellybeans.

Baby ladybugs eat their eggshells.

9

Baby ladybugs
are called larvae.

They eat and grow very fast. Their skin falls off their bodies as they grow.

When a ladybug larva is fully grown, it sticks its body to a leaf.

This is called the pupa stage of the life cycle.

Pupae move very little. They do not eat.

A ladybug changes color and shape when it is a pupa.

Then, its old skin falls off one last time.

An adult ladybug is in the imago stage of the life cycle.

It has two wings.

A hard shell keeps the wings safe.

Female ladybugs lay their **eggs** in a safe place.

A female ladybug will lay up to **2,000 eggs** in her life.

There are about 5,000 kinds of ladybugs.

Each kind has a different color and number of spots.

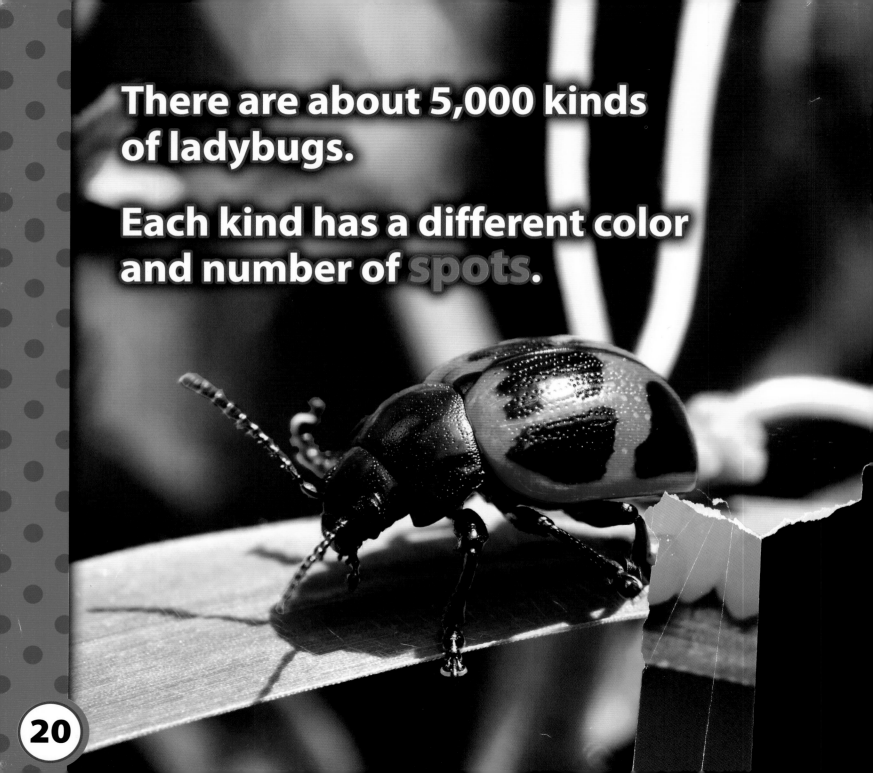

A ladybug larva will grow and change to look the same as its parents.

Life Cycles Quiz

A ladybug's life cycle has four stages.

Larva   Ladybug   Pupa   Egg

Which stage of the life cycle do you see in each picture?

Egg

Ladybug

Pupa

Larva

23

KEY WORDS

Research has shown that as much as 65 percent of all written material published in English is made up of 300 words. These 300 words cannot be taught using pictures or learned by sounding them out. They must be recognized by sight. This book contains 55 common sight words to help young readers improve their reading fluency and comprehension. This book also teaches young readers several important content words, such as proper nouns. These words are paired with pictures to aid in learning and improve understanding.

Page	Sight Words First Appearance
4	a, all, and, animals, grow, have, is, life, this
6	an, are, has, its, of, on, small, the, with
8	from, like, look
9	eat, their
11	as, off, they, very
12	it, to, when
13	do, little, move, not
14	changes
15	last, old, one, then, time
16	in
17	hard, keeps, two
19	her, place, up, will
20	about, different, each, kinds, number, there
21	same

Page	Content Words First Appearance
4	babies, life cycle
6	body, insects, ladybugs, legs, skeleton
8	eggs, jellybeans
9	eggshells
10	larvae
11	skin
12	leaf, pupa stage
14	color, shape
16	imago stage
17	shell, wings
20	spots
21	parents

Published by AV2
350 5th Avenue, 59th Floor New York, NY 10118
Website: www.av2books.com

Library of Congress Cataloging-in-Publication Data
Names: Carr, Aaron, author.
Title: Ladybugs / Aaron Carr.
Description: New York : AV2, [2021] | Series: Exploring life cycles |
   Audience: Ages 4-8 | Audience: Grades K-1
Identifiers: LCCN 2020011836 (print) | LCCN 2020011837 (ebook) | ISBN
   9781791127206 (library binding) | ISBN 9781791127213 (paperback) | ISBN
   9781791127220 | ISBN 9781791127237
Subjects: LCSH: Ladybugs--Juvenile literature.

Classification: LCC QL596.C65 C372 2021 (print) | LCC QL596.C65 (ebook) |
   DDC 595.76/9--dc23
LC record available at https://lccn.loc.gov/2020011836
LC ebook record available at https://lccn.loc.gov/2020011837

Printed in Guangzhou, China
1 2 3 4 5 6 7 8 9 0 24 23 22 21 20

042020
100919

Art Director: Terry Paulhus Project Coordinator: John Willis

Every reasonable effort has been made to trace ownership and to obtain permission to reprint copyright material. The publisher would be pleased to have any errors or omissions brought to its attention so that they may be corrected in subsequent printings.

The publisher acknowledges Getty Images and iStock as the primary image suppliers for this title.